In Our Backyard

How 3 L.A. Neighborhoods Affect Kids' Lives

Anne R. Pebley
Mary E. Vaiana

RAND

Library of Congress Cataloging-in-Publication Data

Pebley, Anne R., 1953–
    In our backyard : how 3 L.A. neighborhoods affect kids' lives / Anne R. Pebley,
Mary E. Vaiana.
        p. cm.
    "MR-1470."
    ISBN 0-8330-3204-6
    1. Children—California—Los Angeles—Social conditions. 2. Child development—
California—Los Angeles. 3. Neighborhood—California—Los Angeles. 4. Community
life—California—Los Angeles. I. Vaiana, Mary E. II.Title.

HQ792.C (California)+
305.23'09794'94—dc21

                                                                          2002068040

Book design by Eileen Delson La Russo

Published 2002 by RAND
1700 Main Street, P.O. Box 2138, Santa Monica, CA 90407-2138
1200 South Hayes Street, Arlington, VA 22202-5050
201 North Craig Street, Suite 202, Pittsburgh, PA 15213-1516
RAND URL: http://www.rand.org/
To order RAND documents or to obtain additional information, contact Distribution
Services: Telephone: (310) 451-7002; Fax: (310) 451-6915; Email: order@rand.org

Preface

This book is intended for a general audience interested in learning more about the subtle interaction between children's well-being and the neighborhoods in which they grow up. The book should also be of interest to community groups, health services agencies, and other groups that want to support children by improving their environment.

Our discussion is based on information drawn from the Focused Study of Children and Neighborhoods (FSCN), a survey of three neighborhoods in Los Angeles conducted in 1998. Unless otherwise noted, all of the tables and graphs in the text are based on data from the 91 families included in that survey. We also used information from the survey to construct the highlighted vignettes of children. These vignettes are composites of real children, but they do not represent any particular child.

The endnotes provide references and more details about the FSCN. For readers who want to know more about the topics in this report, we provide a list for further reading.

Acknowledgments

The Focused Study of Children and Neighborhoods, on which this book is based, was supported by a grant from the W. M. Keck Foundation and by a generous gift from Jane and Ronald L. Olson. However, the authors are solely responsible for all statements and any errors made in this publication.

We are also grateful to our RAND colleagues Eileen La Russo, whose innovative page design gracefully links graphics and text, and Sandra Petitjean, who produced the book's graphics. Christina Pitcher edited the text. The book was enhanced by the thoughtful comments of our technical reviewers, Jill Cannon and Lynn Karoly.

The RAND Survey Research Group conducted the fieldwork for this study, under the capable direction of Jennifer Hawes-Dawson. We would also like to thank Robert Reville, Chris Fair, Shirley Nederend, Mary Lou Gilbert, Audrey Tatum, Roberto Guevara, and Victoria Beard for their participation in this project.

In Our Backyard

How 3 L.A. Neighborhoods Affect Kids' Lives

Why care about neighborhoods?

People love to talk about their neighborhoods, and everyone is an expert on the topic. They have definite opinions about the kinds of people who live in the neighborhood, the kinds of houses they live in, and how much money residents make. They know if their neighborhood is safe or dangerous—and if the latter, where and when. They have definite opinions about the neighborhood's boundaries—the streets or businesses that they think constitute its edges. But each resident may have a slightly different notion of these boundaries, and boundaries may change depending on what a resident is doing—going to work, shopping, or going to religious services. And all of these notions of boundaries may differ from how the U.S. Census Bureau defines the neighborhood.

Residents also feel that neighborhoods affect children's welfare. Sociologists and other scholars agree. Safer neighborhoods, how much contact neighbors have with each other, whether they are willing to assume responsibility for each other and for the neighborhood's children in an emergency, how involved residents are in local organizations— these and other characteristics of a child's environment seem to be associated with kids who are healthier and less likely to have problems at school or at home.

Given the potential nature and size of these effects, it is no exaggeration to think of neighborhoods as the foundation on which the basic social and economic structure of society is built. The sidebar on the following page lists some common beliefs about how neighborhoods influence children.[1] All of these ideas make sense, but the available evidence on each is limited.

> **It is no exaggeration to think of neighborhoods as the foundation on which the basic social and economic structure of society is built.**

Some Common Ideas About How Neighborhoods Affect Children

- *Contagion:* Problem behavior is spread by peer influences

- *Neighbors as role models:* Adults other than parents serve as role models

- *Neighborhood institutions:* Schools, churches, day-care centers, after-school programs are the key

- *Relative deprivation:* Kids may be better off in neighborhoods where others are of the same socioeconomic status

- *Negative effects of a stressful environment:* More stressful neighborhoods result in poorer parenting

In our work, we set out to answer two basic questions:

- What exactly is a neighborhood?
- Which *particular* characteristics of neighborhoods are important for kids?

It's relatively easy to begin answering the first question in older and more densely populated cities such as New York, Boston, or Chicago. In these cities, neighborhoods have been established for a longer time and tend to be relatively stable. And they have been studied a great deal. But the question is more complex in a city like Los Angeles. L.A. is the largest and most important example of a new type of environment increasingly common in the southwest—for example, Phoenix and San Diego. Spread out over a wide area, the urban landscape includes many separate city centers. It's not clear that lessons learned from studying neighborhoods in New York or Boston are applicable to cities like L.A.

Understanding how the individual characteristics of neighborhoods affect kids is a complicated undertaking. Take the example of a study of teenagers in Chicago that concludes that less juvenile delinquency and violence occurs in neighborhoods with trees and green space. Why is that true? It may be that children's physical surroundings have direct effects on their behavior. However, poor neighborhoods that have more trees are also likely to be different from other poor neighborhoods in many ways. For example, they may have active community development groups, more involved residents, and better after-school programs for children.

Figuring out which neighborhood characteristics make a difference in children's development isn't just a matter of academic interest. For example, in the Chicago study mentioned above, unless we understand the underlying reason for the association between trees

and children's behavior, we may draw seriously misleading conclusions and take actions, such as tree-planting programs, which in the end have little effect and reduce potential resources or support for programs that might be effective.

We recently took a close look at three neighborhoods in Los Angeles County to learn more about the link between neighborhood characteristics and the quality of children's lives. Our work provides a rare window on the patterns of daily living in these geographically close, yet rather different worlds.

Hitting the streets in L.A.

Los Angeles provides an ideal laboratory for studying neighborhoods and children because the neighborhoods within the county are tremendously diverse—in ethnicity, social class, governmental structure, school systems, employment, and even terrain. We chose the neighborhoods for our investigation carefully to represent a wide range of experiences. The map on page 4 shows the general areas we selected, but in fact we examined only one census tract in each area. (A census tract is a relatively small area containing 3,000–6,000 people.) The specific census tracts we chose must remain confidential to protect the residents, but we'll use the names of the larger areas—Culver Marina, East L.A., and Windsor View—as a convenient way to refer to the neighborhoods.

> **How do you listen to the heartbeat of a neighborhood? The most obvious answer is "hit the streets."**

How do you listen to the heartbeat of a neighborhood? The most obvious answer is "hit the streets." We drove and walked around the neighborhoods, talked to residents, and visited local businesses. We recorded what we saw, creating a detailed picture of physical characteristics of the neighborhood and daily life within it.

Then we conducted a survey of residents. We gathered information about the lives, opinions, and experiences of about 30 individual families in each neighborhood. For example, we asked questions about how long people had lived in the neighborhood, whether they had close friends and family living nearby, and how safe they thought the neighborhood was. We inquired about their income and their commuting distance to work, shopping, and schools. We asked residents to define the boundaries of their neighborhood and to tell us how responsible they felt for the behavior of neighborhood children.

Location of Study Areas in Los Angeles County

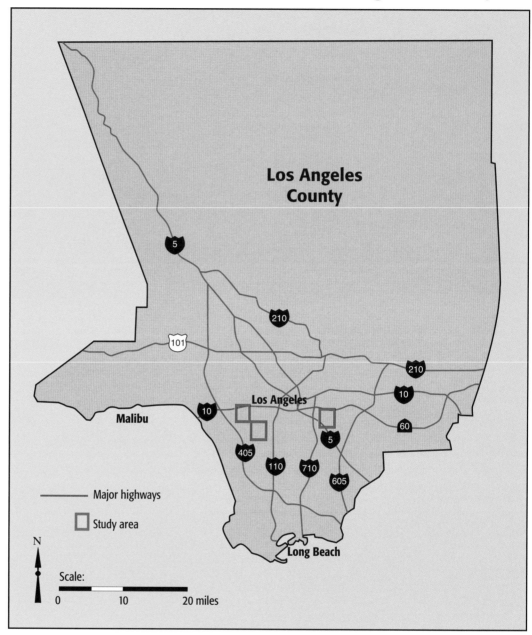

To learn about how neighborhoods and family life affect children, we talked with the adult in each household who had primary responsibility for taking care of the children—in most households this was the mother. We randomly chose one child in the household and asked about the child's health, friends, school performance, and general mood.

To fill in the picture, we talked to shopkeepers and social service agencies such as after-school programs and recreation centers. More information about how we conducted the survey appears at the end of this book.

Community profiles

L.A. is a city dramatically shaped by immigration. The 2000 Census documents sweeping changes in Southern California, as Latinos and Asians have displaced whites and African Americans. But each community, reflecting its own history, echoes the general pattern in its own idiosyncratic way.

Culver Marina is located in the western portion of Los Angeles. The area was part of Rancho La Ballona before U.S. annexation of California. Rancho La Ballona was sold and subdivided by real estate developers beginning in the 1880s. Real estate development accelerated during the 1920s and 1930s. During this period, the Culver Marina neighborhood also began to attract investment by movie studios and maritime-oriented light industry.

The Culver Marina neighborhood originally attracted primarily white middle-income families; however, more recently it has become a very ethnically diverse area, attracting Latino and African American families as well as, more recently, immigrants from Latin America and Asia. The neighborhood is primarily residential although there are several commercial retail and small-scale industrial areas in or near the neighborhood. The residential areas consist mostly of moderate-density single-family dwellings. Parts of this neighborhood are overlaid by major freeways and large boulevards. However, despite the substantial commercial, industrial, and freeway development in the area, the Culver Marina neighborhood still retains the feeling of a suburban community where children play football in the street and neighbors sit out in their front yards in the evening.

Neighborhood Profile—Susan

Susan is 9 years old and lives with her parents, Emily and John. Susan's parents are Filipino immigrants who arrived in the United States in the early 1980s. At home they speak English and Tagalog. Susan was born in Los Angeles.

Susan's father and mother are both college graduates. Her mother works as a medical technician and her father as a sales manager. Her parents' combined income is about $150,000 per year. The family has lived in Culver Marina for about three years. They moved to Los Angeles from Seattle. They have a number of other family members in the neighborhood and many good friends as well. The family is active in their church and in a soccer club. John also regularly works out at the neighborhood YMCA.

Susan attends a private elementary school in her neighborhood. She does very well in school, mostly getting A's. Her parents report few behavior problems at home or at school. Susan is generally a happy and cheerful, though quiet, child.

Susan's health is generally very good. She is covered by health insurance from her mother's job and had a medical checkup about a year ago.

Immigration has shaped these communities in different ways

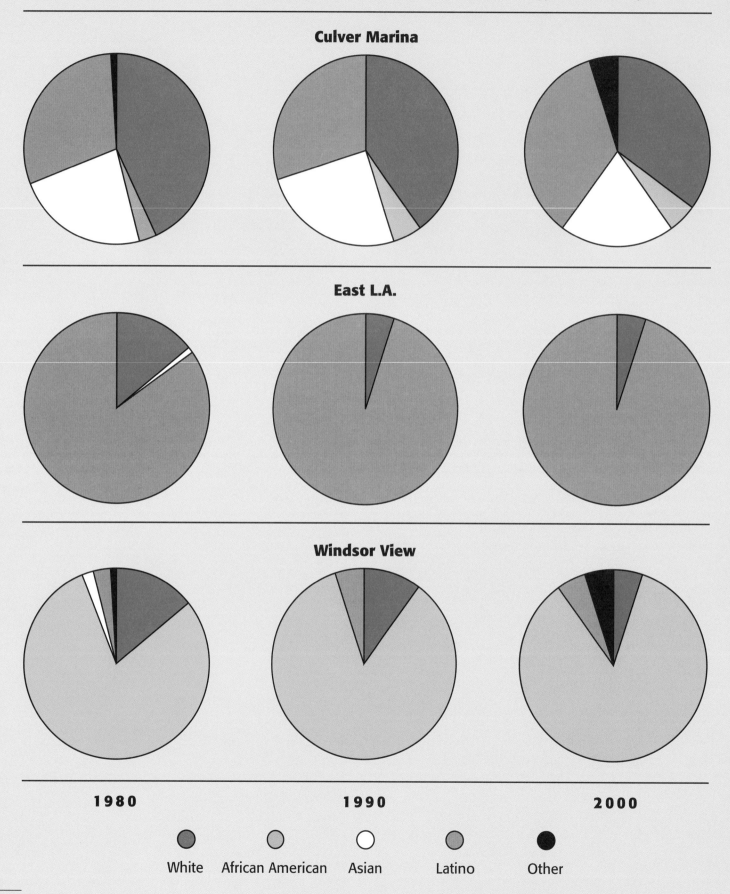

Culver Marina

East L.A.

Windsor View

1980   **1990**   **2000**

⬤ White   ⬤ African American   ◯ Asian   ⬤ Latino   ⬤ Other

[Culver Marina] has a small-town feel that seems out of place on the trendy Westside . . . but residents are fiercely proud of their turf.
        —*L.A. Times*, April 26, 1996, Home Edition, Metro section, Part B, p. 2.

East L.A. is located east of downtown Los Angeles. During much of the 19th century, the land in this area was used for farming, initially by Spaniards and Mexicans and subsequently by American migrants from the Midwest and other parts of the United States. Residential development gradually pushed out agriculture beginning in the late 19th century and early 20th century.

At the beginning of the twentieth century, East Los Angeles became a popular immigrant destination. In the early 1900s, Russians, Jews, Japanese, and Mexicans all had a significant presence in the area. Living east of the river and working in nearby factories, or traveling by electric rail into downtown Los Angeles, immigrants and their children helped fuel the prosperity of the growing metropolis. By the onset of World War II, East Los Angeles was a nearly exclusively Latino community, soon reinforced by Mexican workers who arrived to man the machines in the area's burgeoning war industries. Although the face of the city of Los Angeles and its surrounding communities has changed considerably, East Los Angeles has maintained this basic character throughout the last sixty years.
        —County of Los Angeles Public Library web site, www.colapublib.org/history/eastla/, accessed May 17, 2002.

The population of East L.A. now includes Latino families who have lived in Los Angeles for many generations as well as recent arrivals from Mexico. The East L.A. neighborhood consists primarily of single-family homes and some apartments near commercial retail areas and factories in which many East L.A. residents work.

In East L.A., the front yard is the focus, a place of wrought-iron gates and colorful roses, where neighbors gather on the porch and talk across the fence.
        —*L.A. Times*, Sept. 2, 1999, Home Edition, Southern California Living section, Part E, p. 1, View Desk.

Windsor View is located west of downtown Los Angeles. The first Spanish settlements in the area were *ranchos* in the early 1800s. As happened elsewhere in the Los Angeles basin, most of the *ranchos* were sold to real estate developers and subdivided for housing developments during the 1880s. Rail lines from downtown were built to allow residents to commute to work and shopping. However, in the Windsor View area, agriculture also remained important until well into the early 20th century.

During the 1940s and 1950s, the Windsor View neighborhood and surrounding communities were developed with single-family homes. During the 1950s and 1960s, Japanese Americans and African Americans began moving into the single-family homes in the area, and a thriving residential and commercial community developed in part of this neighborhood. The arrival of Japanese Americans and African Americans in Windsor View was an important landmark in Los Angeles history because it broke the ethnic exclusion barriers that had previously limited settlement in western Los Angeles to whites only.

Most of the development of the Windsor View neighborhood took place during the 1950s and 1960s. Subsequent residential development has generally taken the form of subdivision of single-family homes into multifamily apartments. During the 1970s, Japanese Americans and whites began to move from Windsor View to other areas of the city. As a result of this transition and of in-migration by middle-class African American professionals and their families, Windsor View today is a middle- and upper-income African American neighborhood where most residents have lived for several years and own their own homes.

Neighborhood Profile—Andrew

Andrew, age 8, lives with his parents and 3-year-old brother in Windsor View. His family is African American, and his parents were born in Los Angeles. Both of his parents are college graduates and have good jobs. The family's annual income is about $130,000.

The family has lived in Windsor View for about two years. They moved to the neighborhood because it is very safe and offered nicer housing within their price range. Andrew's mother's job is about 10 minutes away from home, but Andrew's father commutes about half an hour to work.

Andrew attends a private school about 20 minutes away from home. His mother says he does very well in school and has very few behavior problems at school or at home.

Andrew has a lot of friends, but most do not live in his neighborhood. Part of the reason is that many friends attend the same private school but live in other neighborhoods. Nonetheless, friends come to Andrew's house frequently, generally driven over and picked up by their parents.

Andrew has been covered since birth by health insurance provided by his father's employer. His mother says he is in excellent health, although he had problems with allergies and asthma a few years ago. His last medical checkup was four months ago.

The human landscape

Among the neighborhood characteristics that researchers and specialists in child development think are important for children are the age of the community's residents, their incomes, and residential turnover in the neighborhood. Our three neighborhoods differ substantially on all three dimensions.

Age

Since 1970, all three neighborhoods have changed markedly in terms of age structure, mirroring major demographic trends in Los Angeles and in the United States as a whole, but also reflecting the unique experience of each community. These changes are highlighted in the bar charts on the following pages.

For each community, there are four sets of bars showing the demographic makeup of its population based on the U.S. Census in 1970, 1980, 1990, and 1997 (the most recent year for which Census data are currently available). The bars highlight three stages of life. The lowest bars on each graph show children up to 19 years of age. The middle bars include working-age adults, ages 20 to 64, who shoulder the primary responsibility for raising children and earning income to support their families. At the top of the graph are senior citizens, defined here as people age 65 and older. Many senior citizens are retired from the workforce, although they can play an important role in their neighborhoods through activities such as volunteering and helping to care for grandchildren. Looking down a column of bars in the graphs provides a comparison snapshot of the population's age in the three communities at a point in time. Looking across a row of bars gives a sense of how the age structure in a given community has changed over the past 30 years.

> **Since 1970, Windsor View has been the "oldest" of the three neighborhoods.**

Since 1970, Windsor View has been the "oldest" of the three neighborhoods—that is, Windsor View residents have, on average, been older than residents of Culver Marina and East L.A. In 1970, the average age of Windsor View residents was about 37 years. As the graph for 1970 shows, a large proportion of adult Windsor View residents were ages 35 to 64, reflecting the higher incomes and larger

Major Demographic Shifts, 1970–1997

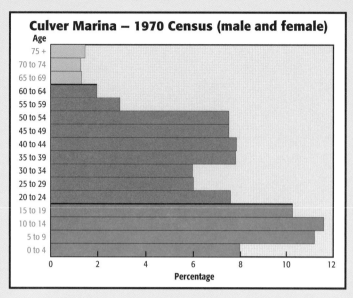

Culver Marina – 1970 Census (male and female)

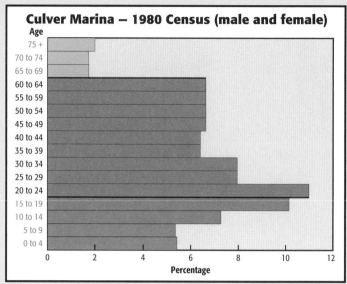

Culver Marina – 1980 Census (male and female)

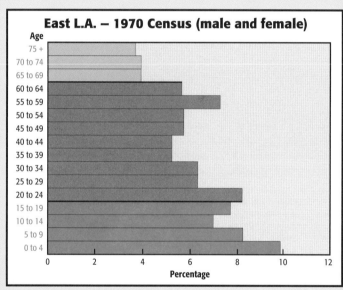

East L.A. – 1970 Census (male and female)

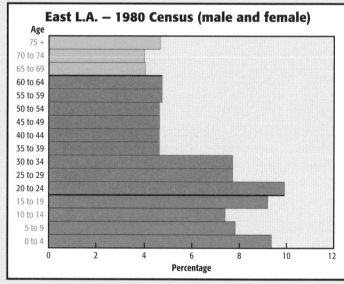

East L.A. – 1980 Census (male and female)

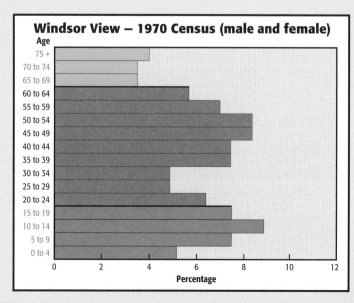

Windsor View – 1970 Census (male and female)

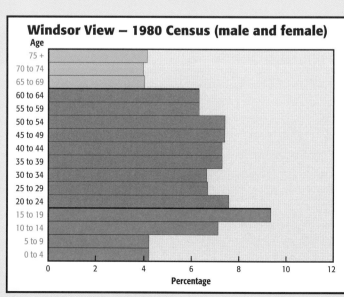

Windsor View – 1980 Census (male and female)

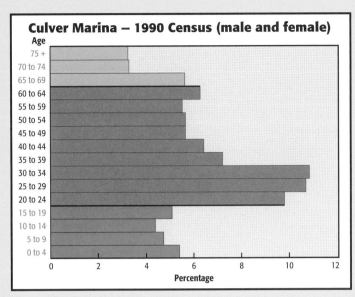

Culver Marina – 1990 Census (male and female)

Age

75 +	
70 to 74	
65 to 69	
60 to 64	
55 to 59	
50 to 54	
45 to 49	
40 to 44	
35 to 39	
30 to 34	
25 to 29	
20 to 24	
15 to 19	
10 to 14	
5 to 9	
0 to 4	

0   2   4   6   8   10   12
Percentage

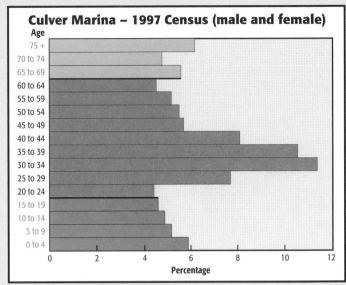

Culver Marina – 1997 Census (male and female)

Age

75 +	
70 to 74	
65 to 69	
60 to 64	
55 to 59	
50 to 54	
45 to 49	
40 to 44	
35 to 39	
30 to 34	
25 to 29	
20 to 24	
15 to 19	
10 to 14	
5 to 9	
0 to 4	

0   2   4   6   8   10   12
Percentage

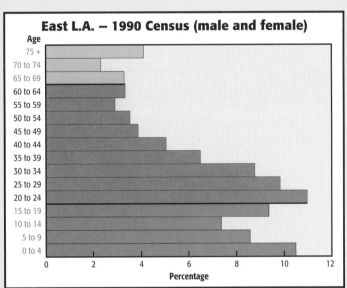

East L.A. – 1990 Census (male and female)

Age

75 +	
70 to 74	
65 to 69	
60 to 64	
55 to 59	
50 to 54	
45 to 49	
40 to 44	
35 to 39	
30 to 34	
25 to 29	
20 to 24	
15 to 19	
10 to 14	
5 to 9	
0 to 4	

0   2   4   6   8   10   12
Percentage

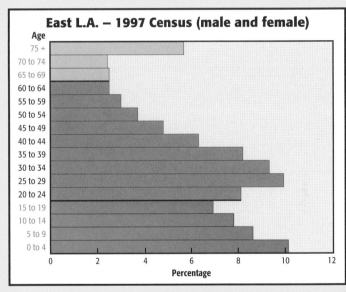

East L.A. – 1997 Census (male and female)

Age

75 +	
70 to 74	
65 to 69	
60 to 64	
55 to 59	
50 to 54	
45 to 49	
40 to 44	
35 to 39	
30 to 34	
25 to 29	
20 to 24	
15 to 19	
10 to 14	
5 to 9	
0 to 4	

0   2   4   6   8   10   12
Percentage

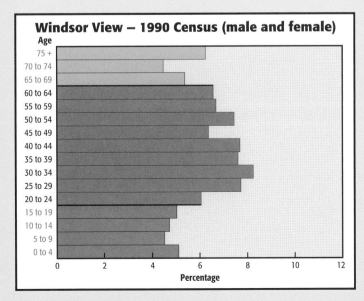

Windsor View – 1990 Census (male and female)

Age

75 +	
70 to 74	
65 to 69	
60 to 64	
55 to 59	
50 to 54	
45 to 49	
40 to 44	
35 to 39	
30 to 34	
25 to 29	
20 to 24	
15 to 19	
10 to 14	
5 to 9	
0 to 4	

0   2   4   6   8   10   12
Percentage

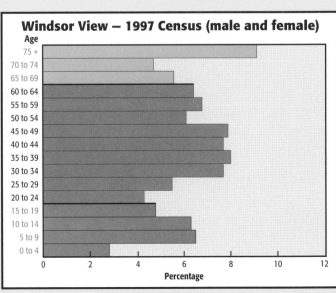

Windsor View – 1997 Census (male and female)

Age

75 +	
70 to 74	
65 to 69	
60 to 64	
55 to 59	
50 to 54	
45 to 49	
40 to 44	
35 to 39	
30 to 34	
25 to 29	
20 to 24	
15 to 19	
10 to 14	
5 to 9	
0 to 4	

0   2   4   6   8   10   12
Percentage

savings required to purchase a house or condo in this neighborhood. The 1970 graph also shows that, like the rest of the United States, Windsor View participated in the post–World War II baby boom, which lasted into the mid-1960s. As a result, by 1970, a large proportion of children living in Windsor View had been born during the baby boom.

In the intervening years, the population of Windsor View has become even older: In 1997, the average age of Windsor View residents was about 43 years. This aging process probably took place in three ways: (1) people who stayed in Windsor View during this entire period began to have fewer children (like the rest of the U.S. population after about 1970) and subsequently became older themselves, (2) families with younger children were less likely to move into Windsor View because housing there is more expensive than in other neighborhoods, and (3) middle-aged and older adults *without* children (either "empty-nesters" or adults who did not have children), who could more easily afford Windsor View housing prices, were more likely to move into the neighborhood.

As a result, only about 20 percent of Windsor View residents in 1997 were under the age of 20. And the ratio of children to seniors (the number of children 19 and younger divided by the number of seniors 65 and older) was about 1 to 1—in other words, there were about equal numbers of seniors and children in Windsor View in 1997. During the time we spent in Windsor View, it became apparent that there were far fewer children in this neighborhood than in the other two. It was more difficult to locate families with children, and interviewers observing neighborhood life rarely saw children playing outside or going to school. In addition, as we will see later on, Windsor View is a very stable neighborhood, where neighbors have often known each other for years. Therefore, although children in Windsor View are less likely to find other children of their own age to play with in their neighborhood, they may grow up knowing more adult neighbors in a supportive environment.

Reflecting a national trend, the number of residents age 75 and older grew rapidly in Windsor View during this more recent period. Throughout the United States, these older seniors have benefited from substantial declines in mortality and increases in life expectancy.

Culver Marina has experienced even more dramatic aging of its population than Windsor View. In 1970, the average age of Culver Marina residents was about

29 years, the youngest of all three neighborhoods. As the graph for 1970 shows, the age structure of the population was dominated by children, in part because of the nationwide baby boom during the 1950s and 1960s, and also because of the availability of low-cost housing for young families in this newly developed area. The Culver Marina neighborhood was a very "child-friendly" place in which children could easily find friends their own age to play with. At the other end of the age spectrum, there were few seniors in Culver Marina in 1970, because Culver Marina was developed relatively recently and attracted primarily younger families.

As the bar charts show, since 1970 the number of children has declined as a proportion of the population of Culver Marina, while the number of seniors has increased markedly. Culver Marina has changed from a recently developed residen-

> **The Culver Marina neighborhood was a very "child-friendly" place in which children could easily find friends their own age to play with.**

Neighborhood Profile—Samantha

Samantha, age 6, lives with her 33-year-old aunt Hope and her 70-year-old grandparents, Jordan and Carol. Jordan, who is Samantha's legal guardian, identifies her ethnicity as multiracial. Like his own, it includes African American, white, and Native American ancestors.

Samantha's grandfather completed two years of college and worked for most of his life in a manufacturing plant but is now retired, as is his wife. The family's income comes primarily from Social Security payments, Jordan's veteran's pension, income from rental property, and Hope's salary.

Jordan and Carol have lived in Windsor View for 35 years. Samantha's mother used to live with them, but moved to Chicago several years ago. When Samantha was born, her mother was having financial and health problems. She took Samantha to live with her grandparents, where she has lived ever since.

Family life is generally happy. No other family members live in the neighborhood, but there are lots of friends around. The family has visitors several times a week.

Samantha entered her local public elementary school last year. Her grandfather reports that she has few behavior problems and gets mostly A's.

The family is moderately involved in neighborhood activities, often at their neighborhood church. Carol sometimes takes Samantha to the library for story hour. Family members all enjoy reading and have many books and magazines at home.

Neighborhood Profile—Casey

Casey is 16 years old and lives with her 45-year-old father Jim. Jim is divorced from Casey's mother and has custody. Casey and Jim are white and have lived in Culver Marina since the divorce, about five years.

Jim is a high school graduate who is currently unemployed. His most recent job was as a police officer. The family income this year has been about $65,000, and Jim and Casey are living primarily off of Jim's savings and investments. Jim expects to have another job very soon.

As a single father, it hasn't been easy for Jim to raise Casey, especially since he has been unemployed. He reports that they argue quite a bit and that Casey has serious behavior problems at home.

Casey attends a public school about four miles from her home. Although Jim reports that she is not considered to have problem behavior at school, she has been suspended a few times. She has also skipped school a few times without permission. Her school performance has not been very good either: She gets primarily C's. Despite these problems, the school has not asked Jim to meet with Casey's teachers or principal during the past 12 months to talk over Casey's problems.

Casey has about five close friends but brings them home only occasionally. None of the friends live in her neighborhood.

tial area settled predominantly by young families with children to a more rooted and older neighborhood in which middle-aged adults and seniors have come to dominate the population. By 1997, the average age of Culver Marina residents was 39 years, a full 10 years older than the average in 1970. However, unlike Windsor View, Culver Marina still has more children under age 20 than seniors age 65 and over: The ratio is 1.2 children per senior, compared with only 1 child per senior in Windsor View.

Rather than aging, the population of the East L.A. neighborhood actually became younger between 1970 and 1997: The average age declined from 35 years in 1970 to 32 years in 1997. The change occurred primarily because of an influx of young adults and their children into this neighborhood. Some of these young families were recent immigrants, while others were native Angelenos who wanted to take advantage of the neighborhood's lower housing and rental prices. The graphs also show the effects of a slightly higher birth rate in East L.A. than in the other two neighborhoods.

Because of these changes in age structure, the ratio of children to seniors in East L.A. was very high. For every senior age 65 and older, there were *three* children under age 20. As we noted above, the majority of working-age adults in East L.A. was also relatively young compared with the other two neighborhoods in the study. As a result, residents of the East L.A. neighborhood were primarily young families with children.

Income

Windsor View was the wealthiest of the three neighborhoods, and, not surprisingly, its residents were the best educated, since education and income tend to be closely connected. A substantial number of families had incomes above $100,000 a year and had four years of post–high school education. In contrast, almost all families in East L.A. had incomes below $50,000 a year and a high school education. Culver Marina fell between the other two neighborhoods in terms of income and education, but residents in both Culver Marina and East L.A. were significantly less likely than their Windsor View counterparts to say that they were better off than the average Californian.

Income differences can drive important decisions that parents make for the sake of their children. We asked parents if they had ever done the following things to make life better for their kids: (a) moved to a different neighborhood, (b) increased work hours or taken a second job, and (c) reduced their work hours or refused extra work.

Parents in Windsor View were significantly more likely to have moved and to have reduced their work hours. These middle-class parents could afford to move to

> **Windsor View was the wealthiest of the three neighborhoods, and, not surprisingly, its residents were the best educated.**

What parents in these communities have done to make life better for their children

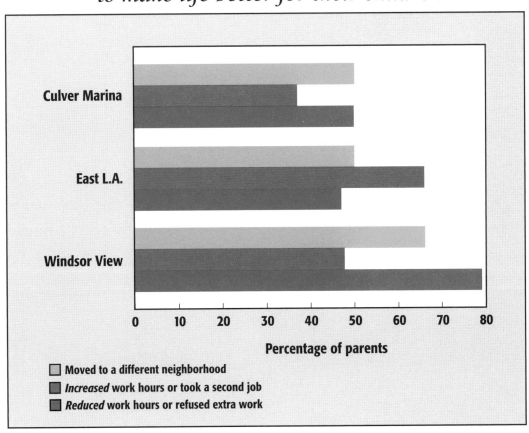

Percentage of parents

☐ Moved to a different neighborhood
■ *Increased* work hours or took a second job
■ *Reduced* work hours or refused extra work

a better neighborhood and work less so that they could stay home with their kids. Like other middle-class parents, they often feel that spending more time with their children is the best way to improve their children's well-being. In contrast, parents in East L.A. were more likely to have increased their work hours or taken a second job. East L.A. parents were less likely to be able to afford to move to a better neighborhood than were parents in Windsor View. Since these families are poorer, they are more likely to feel that bringing home more money is the best way to improve their kids' lives.

Residential turnover

Given the average financial status of residents in each of the three neighborhoods, it is not surprising that Windsor View had the lowest proportion of renters, while East L.A. had the highest. Common sense suggests that families are more likely to remain in neighborhoods and to invest their time and energy in their neighborhoods when they own their own homes—primarily because they feel they have a greater stake in the neighborhood.

However, results from our study show that residential turnover is not always closely related to home ownership. For example, residential stability (defined as the percentage of our respondents living in the same home for more than five years) was lowest in Culver Marina, but East L.A. had a smaller proportion of home owners than Culver Marina. Residential stability was very high in Windsor View, where about three-quarters of residents owned their own homes, but it was also high in East L.A., with half of the residents living in the same home for at least five years.

> **Families who own their own home have a greater stake in the neighborhood.**

Residential Stability Is Not Always Related to Home Ownership		
Neighborhood	Percentage of families owning their home	Percentage of families living in same home for 5+ years
Culver Marina	63	37
East L.A.	48	50
Windsor View	72	69

How big is a child's neighborhood?

During our discussions with neighborhood residents, we asked them to tell us how big their neighborhood was. We wanted to know whether there was general agreement about neighborhood boundaries and, if there were differences, what might cause them. We found that residents had very clear ideas about the boundaries of their neighborhoods, but they didn't necessarily agree about where those boundaries lie. In fact, individual residents might define boundaries differently depending on whether they were considering where they shop, where their kids go to school, or where they go to religious services.

To illustrate this variation, we show on page 18 one resident's multiple boundaries, which fan out from the street on which he lived. The smallest boundary was defined by his knowledge of his immediate neighbors and his contact with them. The second boundary was defined by a problem he had with a single resident and the subsequent process of uniting with other residents to cope with the problem. The most expansive boundary was defined through his contact with the police department; this boundary corresponded quite closely to the map displayed at his neighborhood watch meetings. These multiple boundaries reflect the diversity of his personal experience in the neighborhood.

> **Residents had very clear ideas about the boundaries of their neighborhoods, but they didn't necessarily agree about where those boundaries lie.**

Why is it important to understand how people think about their neighborhood's physical dimensions? It matters for the same reason that we want to understand exactly why neighborhoods with trees have less juvenile delinquency. Understanding where most family activities take place helps nonprofit organizations and agencies decide where to focus efforts to improve children's lives. For example, can an after-school program intended to serve a particular neighborhood be ten miles away and still be convenient for parents? Or does it need to be closer? In addition, the expansiveness with which people define their neighborhoods seems to go hand in hand with how responsible they feel personally for others who live in the neighborhood, including children.

From our discussions with residents, we learned that there is a great deal of variation in how people who live in the same neighborhood perceive its boundaries. For example, we asked residents in each community to tell us how big they thought their neighborhood was. The figure on the top of page 19 summarizes their answers. Boundary definitions varied both between and within neighborhoods. For example, the majority of people living in the Culver Marina neighborhood said that their neighborhood included the block they live on plus several blocks in each direction. In the Windsor View neighborhood, most residents said that their neighborhood included the area within a 15-minute walk from their house, or an even larger area. East L.A. neighborhood residents gave the broadest range of answers, signaling even less agreement on neighborhood boundaries than in the other two neighborhoods.

A Culver Marina resident's
multiple definitions of his neighborhood

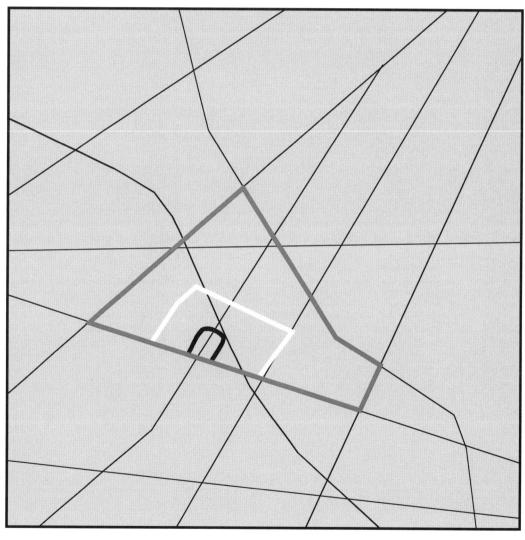

▬▬▬ Day-to-day perception of the neighborhood
☐☐☐ Expanded definition from dealing with problem neighbor
▬▬▬ Boundary defined through participation in Neighborhood Watch

Windsor View residents have the most expansive definition of their neighborhood

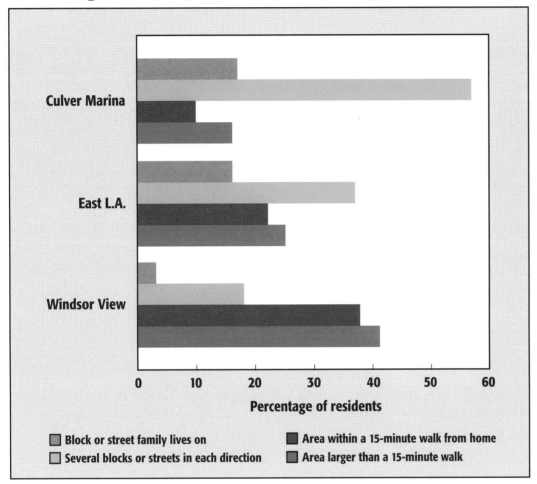

Percentage of residents

- ☐ Block or street family lives on
- ☐ Several blocks or streets in each direction
- ☐ Area within a 15-minute walk from home
- ☐ Area larger than a 15-minute walk

Average Travel Time to Daily Activities

Daily Destination	Culver Marina	East L.A.	Windsor View
Respondent's job	18 minutes	20 minutes	19 minutes
Spouse's employment	18 minutes	17 minutes	20 minutes
Place of worship	11 minutes	12 minutes	13 minutes
Children's school	10 minutes	9 minutes	15 minutes
Children's day care	8 minutes	9 minutes	11 minutes
Grocery store	6 minutes	6 minutes	8 minutes

Despite these differing definitions, the areas surrounding where families live clearly *do* play an important role in residents' daily lives, in all three neighborhoods. Although Los Angeles is well known for hour-long commutes to work, the table on the previous page shows that residents in these neighborhoods generally reported working within 17 to 20 minutes of home. Children's schools and day-care providers, places of worship, and grocery stores were even closer.

The neighborhood environment

What is it like for children to live in these neighborhoods? Experts think that several aspects of neighborhood social environment are particularly important for children, including

- safety
- whether neighbors know each other
- social cohesion—that is, the involvement of adults in monitoring the neighborhood and intervening when necessary.[2]

Safety

Residents of the Culver Marina and East L.A. neighborhoods generally believed their neighborhoods were safe, but virtually *all* residents in Windsor View believed that their neighborhood was safe.

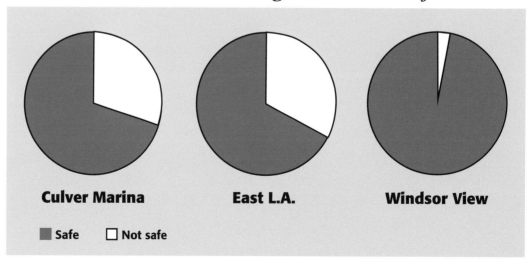

Percentage of residents who think their neighborhood is safe

Culver Marina   East L.A.   Windsor View

■ Safe   □ Not safe

Interaction with neighbors

An important aspect of a neighborhood's social environment is how much regular interaction there is among neighbors. Many studies suggest that if neighbors know and trust each other they are more likely to take action to ensure the safety and well-being of neighbors and the neighborhood. They are also more likely to watch out for neighborhood children and to make sure they are not getting into trouble.

It's not that neighbors need to be good friends and spend a lot of time with each other to create a positive social environment for children. In fact, many "child-friendly" neighborhoods are not necessarily close-knit communities. Rather, it's important that residents know who their neighbors are, have basic trust in them, and share common values.

> **If neighbors know and trust each other, they are more likely to take action to ensure the safety and well-being of neighbors and the neighborhood.**

We looked at several different measures of social interaction in these neighborhoods.

First, we examined what proportion of respondents reported having family members (not including those living in the respondent's own household) or good friends living in the neighborhood. About one-third of respondents in Culver Marina and Windsor View reported that at least one family member lives in their neighborhood. In East L.A., more than half of the respondents reported having family in the neighborhood. Although this may appear surprising given the influx of immigrant families to East L.A. in the 1980s and 1990s, it reflects a long tradition of families living near each other in East L.A. and of recent immigrants settling near family members who arrived earlier.

A majority of respondents reported that they have at least one good friend living in their neighborhood. Neighborhood friendships are easier to form the longer one lives in a neighborhood. Thus, it is not surprising to find that residents in the neighborhood with the least residential stability, Culver Marina, were the least likely to report that they have a good friend in the neighborhood. Windsor View, which has the highest residential stability, also had the highest proportion of respondents reporting that they have at least one good friend in the neighborhood.

Similarly, while respondents in Culver Marina reported talking regularly to about six adults in their neighborhood, residents in East L.A. talked regularly with about seven, and Windsor View residents with more than eight. So residential stability appears to increase both the number of adults residents know in the neighborhood and the chances of having a good friend living there.

Knowing Neighbors

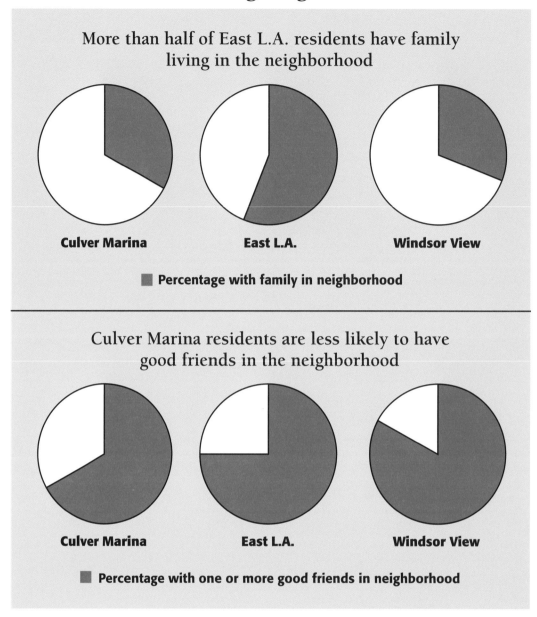

More than half of East L.A. residents have family living in the neighborhood

Culver Marina East L.A. Windsor View

■ Percentage with family in neighborhood

Culver Marina residents are less likely to have good friends in the neighborhood

Culver Marina East L.A. Windsor View

■ Percentage with one or more good friends in neighborhood

By contrast, although respondents in Culver Marina were likely to talk regularly with fewer adults than those in the other two neighborhoods, they talked regularly with more kids than respondents in the other two neighborhoods. Part of the reason, as described above, is that kids are a relatively small proportion of the Windsor View population—there just aren't that many in the neighborhood to talk to. It is less clear why respondents in East L.A. reported talking regularly to fewer kids, on average, than respondents in Culver Marina since, as we have seen, the proportion of children in East L.A. is higher than in either of the other two neighborhoods.

We also asked respondents to answer a standardized set of six questions about the amount of conflict in their families.[3] Despite the very different family circumstances and experiences of respondents in the three neighborhoods, the average level of family conflict reported in each neighborhood was almost identical. Family conflict was about equally common in all three neighborhoods: On average, families in each neighborhood reported a relatively moderate level of conflict (an average of 12 on a scale from 4 to 24).

Social cohesion

Social cohesion reflects the extent to which families in the neighborhood cooperate to keep the neighborhood safe, to keep kids safe and out of trouble, and to prevent crime. The Social Cohesion Index was developed and tested by researchers at Harvard and the University of Chicago to assess the social environment of neighborhoods in Chicago.[4] Respondents were asked eight questions about how likely it is that a neighbor would intervene if he or she observed different types of problems in the neighborhood—for example, a child painting or writing on a car or building. The index ranges from 8, which indicates very low cohesion (i.e., little cooperation or involvement by neighbors), to 32, which indicates very high levels of cohesion.

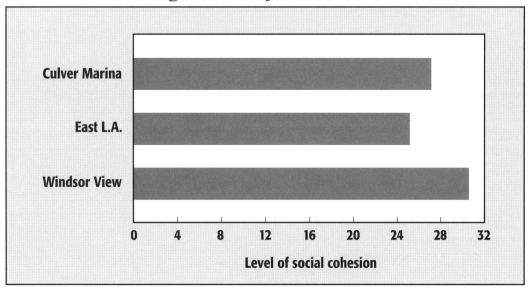

Windsor View residents have high levels of social cohesion

Respondents in all three neighborhoods reported fairly high levels of social cohesion in their neighborhoods. However, Windsor View respondents reported a significantly higher level of social cohesion than did those in the other two neighborhoods. This pattern is consistent with other characteristics of Windsor View that we have mentioned—for example, high residential stability and an expansive definition of what constitutes the residents' neighborhood. The average level of social cohesion in Windsor View is significantly higher statistically than it is in the other two neighborhoods, but the differences are not large.

We also examined the average level of residents' involvement in neighborhood organizations and activities, such as community service groups, religious groups, neighborhood watch programs, and school-related groups. We found relatively high levels of neighborhood involvement in all three neighborhoods. On average, residents in Culver Marina and East L.A. were involved in two to three activities, but the highest involvement was in Windsor View, where, on average, residents were involved in more than three such activities.

Neighborhood Profile—Mariana

Mariana, age 6, lives with her parents and younger sister in East L.A. Her parents immigrated from Mexico in 1990, three years before Mariana was born. Since then, they have moved back and forth between Mexico and the United States several times. The family speaks both English and Spanish at home, but Mariana's mother, Paty, feels most comfortable speaking Spanish. The family has lived in this neighborhood for most of the past ten years.

Mariana's father, Rogelio, works as a computer technician and earns about $30,000 a year. Paty has worked in the past as a waitress but now stays home with the children.

Mariana is in kindergarten. Her performance at school is okay, but could be better. When she first entered school, she was placed in a bilingual education program. Since then, her English has improved, and she is now in a regular kindergarten class.

Her mother reports that Mariana has many behavior problems at home. Sometimes she has behavior problems at school as well — she is frequently distracted and doesn't pay attention. Paty has met with Mariana's teacher twice this year to discuss the problem.

During the past month, Mariana's mother attended a church club meeting, visited a neighbor, and went to the library's story hour with Mariana's little sister.

How well are kids doing in these neighborhoods?

We looked at several indicators of how children are doing in the three neighborhoods.

Behavior

To look at behavior, we used the Behavior Problems Index (BPI), a well-tested, standardized set of questions used in many national surveys, to determine the level of children's behavior problems. The questions cover about 30 behavior traits—for example, "(He/she) cheats or tells lies," and "(He/she) has difficulty concentrating." The BPI ranges from 0, meaning no problems, to 33, meaning that a child has lots of problems.

In general, parents in all three neighborhoods reported that their children have relatively few behavior problems. In both Culver Marina and Windsor View, children's average score was just over 7 on the BPI. However, parents reported significantly more behavior problems for their children in East L.A., where the average score was over 12.

Part of the difference between the neighborhoods could be due to language and perhaps to cultural differences. Parents who were bilingual in English and Spanish or who spoke only Spanish were more likely to report that their children had behavior problems. However, there appears to be a neighborhood effect as well. Even when we eliminated the effects of language, parents in East L.A. reported more behavior problems than did parents in Culver Marina. For example, when we compared bilingual (English/Spanish) parents in Culver Marina with those in East L.A., parents in East L.A. were still more likely to report more behavior problems. The same is true when we compared monolingual Spanish-speaking parents in the two neighborhoods. The higher levels of poverty and crime in East L.A. compared to the Culver Marina and Windsor View areas may create more opportunities for kids to develop behavior problems.

Children in these three communities seem to be equally gregarious.

Children in these three communities seem to be equally gregarious. Parents we interviewed reported that their children had, on average, eight to ten friends. But kids in East L.A. were significantly more likely to have friends close by. More than half of their friends lived in the neighborhood.

[Children] have such a facility for making friends . . . they communicate with each other very easily. I say to my kids "From where do you know her?" They tell me "just now I asked of her what her name was . . . and well, now, she is my friend. . ."

—An East L.A. resident

School performance

The majority of kids in all three neighborhoods attended public school, but a substantial minority in Culver Marina and Windsor View—about one-third—attended private schools. In East L.A., few children attended private school. Given the ethnic composition of that community, it's not surprising that about two-thirds of children over 5 years of age had been in a bilingual or bicultural education program, and about one-third had attended classes in English as a second language. Few Culver Marina children and none of the children in Windsor View had ever been in such a class. However about one-quarter of the children in these two neighborhoods had been in a gifted student class or school; children in East L.A. were rarely in such classes.

Indicators of Children's Well-Being

	Culver Marina	East L.A.	Windsor View
Children's behavior Behavior Problems Index (Scale of 0 to 33. Higher score means more behavior problems.)	7.6	12.4	7.4
School performance Parents' assessment (Scale of 1 to 5. Higher score means child is doing better.)	4.0	3.5	4.1
Health Parents' assessment of general health status (Scale of 1 to 5. Higher score means better health.)	4.5	3.8	4.7
% with health insurance	90%	81%	97%
% who had a checkup in past 12 months	23%	25%	45%

Parents were asked to rate how their children were doing in school on a scale of 1 (poor) to 5 (excellent). Children in East L.A. were more likely to perform poorly in school, according to their parents' reports. Reasons for poor school performance are complex. In this case, they are likely to be related to poverty, poorer schools, parenting style, and poorer health service access.

Health

We asked parents to rate their children's overall health status on a scale from 0 (poor) to 5 (excellent). Children in the Windsor View neighborhood were reported to be in the best health, although those in the Culver Marina neighborhood were very close. By contrast, children in the East L.A. neighborhood were reported to be in poorer health.

We also looked at whether children were covered by health insurance and whether they had had a checkup in the past 12 months. Virtually all children in the Windsor View and Culver Marina neighborhoods were covered by health insurance. In contrast, almost 20 percent in the East L.A. neighborhood were *not* covered by any type of health insurance (including MediCal and the Healthy Families program). This difference is most likely explained by the income disparities among residents in the three neighborhoods. Families in the East L.A. neighborhood have lower incomes and are more likely to have jobs that do not include health care benefits. However, the MediCal and Healthy Families programs should cover many of these children.

As other studies have shown, poorer families, particularly immigrant or non-English-speaking families, often do not know that they are eligible for coverage or find the paperwork and procedures daunting. This is likely to account for at least some of the differences between children in the East L.A. neighborhood and those in the other two study areas.

Not surprisingly, only 25 percent of children in the East L.A. neighborhood had a medical checkup in the past 12 months, compared with 45 percent of kids in Windsor View. However, it is also true that only about 25 percent of children in Culver Marina had a checkup, which is somewhat surprising given the relatively high levels of health insurance coverage in this neighborhood.

Part of the difference in the number of children who had regular medical checkups in these communities is undoubtedly due to the fact that children in the Windsor View study area were more likely to have health insurance. However, that factor cannot account for all of the difference in checkups, since most children in the Culver Marina neighborhood also had health insurance.

Which characteristics of neighborhoods are important for children?

We've seen that there are substantial differences in the well-being of children living in these three study neighborhoods. In general, Windsor View children have the best outcomes, children in the East L.A. neighborhood the worst, and those in Culver Marina, somewhere in between. There are some exceptions to this pattern. Only one-quarter of Culver Marina kids have had a medical checkup in the past year, which ranks them about the same as East L.A., compared to almost one-half of children in Windsor View.

Why do the measures of how children are doing differ so much among the three neighborhoods? Part of the answer is likely found in differences in the characteristics of families who live in each neighborhood. For example, families in East

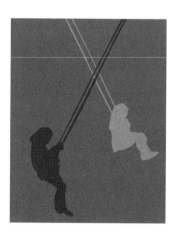

L.A. are more likely to be poor than those in Culver Marina, and families in Windsor View are much better off financially. Poor families are less able to provide high-quality day care when both parents work, to send their children to good schools, to have health insurance, and to afford to take their children for medical checkups. Research also shows that poverty itself is very stressful for families and may lead to less-effective parenting and emotional stress for children.[5]

To determine whether the differences we see among the three neighborhoods in children's well-being are due to differences in income level or to other characteristics of the families in each neighborhood, we conducted a statistical analysis in which we can hold constant, or factor out, differences in family characteristics among the three neighborhoods. For example, we can determine whether there are statistically significant differences in children's health care coverage once we eliminate the effects of income differences between neighborhoods. With the results of this analysis, we can answer questions such as: Would East L.A. children have as many behavior problems if their families were not as poor? Do lower income and a higher likelihood of being an immigrant (rather than native born) reduce the chance that children in East L.A. and Culver Marina will be covered by health insurance?

In addition to income, we can also hold constant other family characteristics that are likely to affect each measure of children's well-being. For example, in the case of the Behavior Problems Index (BPI), we can eliminate the effect of family differences in both income and the amount of conflict reported in the family: Family conflict has been shown in other studies to be associated with children's behavior problems.[6] Another major difference among families is whether other family members live in the neighborhood. Does the presence of other relatives in the neighborhood have a significant effect on children's well-being?

We applied our statistical method to four measures of children's well-being: behavior problems, whether or not the child is covered by health insurance, the child's health status, and how well the child does in school. We will discuss each measure of children's well-being separately, beginning with behavior problems.

Behavior problems

As we have seen, parents in East L.A. reported that their children had significantly more behavior problems than parents in the other two neighborhoods reported. Our analysis shows that Spanish-speaking parents in particular were more likely to report behavior problems than those who were bilingual (English/Spanish) and those who spoke English only. (To gather information from Spanish-speaking parents, we used a well-tested Spanish translation of the BPI questions; RAND's own Spanish-language specialist reviewed the translation.) However, even when we held home language constant, significant differences remained in the frequency of behavior problems between children in East L.A. and those in Culver Marina. We can't make comparisons with Windsor View because there are essentially no Spanish speakers there.

> Low family income and a high level of family conflict are both related to higher levels of problem behaviors for children.

So what accounts for this difference? Our statistical analysis shows that low family income and a high level of family conflict are both related to higher levels of problem behaviors for children. Conversely, children in families who have other relatives in the neighborhood (other than those living in the household) are better off. As we have seen, families in East L.A. are more likely to have other relatives in the neighborhood, but families in all three neighborhoods have about the same level of family conflict. So while children in East L.A. are at a disadvantage because they are more likely to live in a poor family, they also have a significant advantage because they are more likely to have other family members living nearby.

What happens if we use statistical methods to hold constant family income and the number of family members in the neighborhood? We found that children in Culver Marina and Windsor View still have significantly fewer behavior problems than do children in East L.A. This finding suggests that other differences in family characteristics are important and that, regardless of family characteristics, living in a particular neighborhood has an effect on a child's behavior. In fact, our results show that the effects of family characteristics themselves differ by neighborhood—that is, being poor in Culver Marina or Windsor Hills is not the same as being poor in East L.A.

We can explore how family income affects behavior problems in each neighborhood by asking a series of "What if" questions. For example, we asked whether, on average, children living in a family with an income of $25,000 would have the same number of behavior problems as children living in a family with an income of $50,000 or $100,000. The table below shows the answers to our questions.

The first column shows the average BPI in each neighborhood. In East L.A., increases in family income substantially lower the BPI. If we hold everything else constant, we see that East L.A. children from higher-income families ($100,000) have only 38 percent of the behavior problems that children in poorer families ($25,000) have. It appears that higher-income families in East L.A. are able to compensate for some of the negative consequences of living in a poor neighborhood; however, for East L.A. children in lower-income families, the effects of family poverty are compounded by growing up in a poor family. That is, even controlling for family income, children have more behavior problems if they live in East L.A.

In Windsor View, children in upper-income families are also likely to have fewer behavior problems, but the difference between lower- and higher-income chil-

How Income Affects Children's Behavior in These Three Neighborhoods

Neighborhood	Average Behavior Problems Index	Percentage of problems if family income = $25,000	Percentage of problems if family income = $50,000	Percentage of problems if family income = $100,000
Culver Marina	7.6	100	104	112
East L.A.	12.4	100	79	38
Windsor View	7.4	100	96	88
Average across all three neighborhoods	9.13			

dren is substantially less than in East L.A. Children in families making $100,000 (fairly common in Windsor View) have 88 percent of the behavior problems of children in lower-income families.

In Culver Marina, family income has the opposite effect of what would be expected, holding everything else constant. The parents of children in upper-income families are somewhat *more* likely to report that their children have behavior problems than are lower-income parents. The information we have makes it difficult to determine why income has a different, albeit not very large, effect in this neighborhood.

The table below illustrates how children's behavior is affected by having family members (outside the household) living in the same neighborhood. The first column shows the average BPI for each neighborhood. If no other family members live in the neighborhood, the index is unchanged. But if we change the presence of family members, holding income and other characteristics constant, we see a change in the percentage of problems that children have in each neighborhood. For example, children in East L.A. who have six family members in the neighborhood have only 58 percent as many behavior problems as children with no other family members in the neighborhood. In Culver Marina, having other family members in the neighborhood also reduces the chances of having behavior problems, though not as much as in East L.A.

In contrast, in Windsor View, having family members in the neighborhood actually increases the chances of having behavior problems. In this case, the reason may be that in Windsor View, few households have other family members in the neighborhood. Parents who choose to live in the same neighborhood as other family

How Having Other Family Members in the Neighborhood Affects Children's Behavior

Neighborhood	Average Behavior Problems Index	If three other family members in neighborhood (% of problems)	If six other family members in neighborhood (% of problems)
Culver Marina	7.6	94	87
East L.A.	12.4	79	58
Windsor View	7.4	110	121
Average across all three neighborhoods	9.13		

members may do so because they or their children are experiencing problems, such as divorce or separation. Or parents may choose to live near grandparents if they have a child who is particularly difficult to raise. This type of effect may also occur in Culver Marina and East L.A., but may be strongly counteracted by the positive effects of having family in the neighborhood.

Other children's outcomes

We carried out the same type of analysis for other measures of children's well-being described above. For example, in the case of health insurance coverage, family income and immigrant status account for differences in children's health insurance coverage between East L.A. and Culver Marina. However, children in Windsor View are still significantly more likely to be covered by health insurance. This difference is probably due to the fact that parents in Windsor View are more likely to hold professional and managerial occupations, which come with health insurance coverage, than are families in East L.A. and, to a lesser extent, in Culver Marina. Parental occupation remains a very important predictor of children's health insurance coverage throughout Los Angeles, despite the availability of low-cost, publicly subsidized health insurance for children and families (in many cases, without regard to immigrant status) through the Healthy Families and MediCal programs.

> Parents who report that their neighborhood is very safe or fairly safe are more likely to perceive their children to be in good health.

In the case of children's overall health status, we found that differences in family income account for most of the differences in health status between Windsor View and East L.A., but not for differences between Culver Marina and East L.A. We also discovered that parents who report that their neighborhood is very safe or fairly safe are more likely to perceive their children to be in good health than are parents who believe that their neighborhood is not safe. This finding is equally true for all three neighborhoods. Among the greatest threats in Los Angeles to the health of children, especially teenagers, are crime, violence, and automobile accidents.[7] Thus, it is not surprising that parents who perceive their neighborhoods to be safe are less concerned about these types of threats to their children's health. There is also considerable evidence that the stress of living in unsafe neighborhoods may detrimentally affect parents' and children's outlook on life.[8] So families who worry less about safety in their neighborhoods or who live in safer neighborhoods may, in fact, have kids who are in better physical and mental health.

Finally, differences in family income among the three neighborhoods appear to account for *all* of the differences in children's school performance. That is, once family income is held constant, children in all three neighborhoods are reported by parents to be doing equally well in school. Of course, caution is necessary in interpreting this result because parents in different neighborhoods may differ in their expectations of what constitutes "doing well" in school. Nonetheless, the results suggest that upper- and middle-income children in East L.A. may perform about as well in school as children of the same income level in the other two neighborhoods: Family poverty is at least part of the explanation for poor school performance in East L.A.

Learning more about the effects of neighborhoods

We began this discussion by considering the observation that neighborhoods with more trees have less violence and fewer juvenile delinquents. We noted that this fact alone tells us nothing about whether it's the trees that matter or whether the real influence is some other characteristic of neighborhoods that just also happen to have lots of trees.

In our study of three L.A. neighborhoods, we've been able to identify some of the subtle links between children's well-being and characteristics of their families and neighborhoods. We have seen that even in a sprawling and seemingly boundary-less urban area like Los Angeles, neighborhoods are important and salient to their residents. Despite the common perception that Angelenos must drive long distances to get almost anywhere, parents and children in these three neighborhoods spend much of their day fairly close to home. There is also a high level of "neighborliness" in these neighborhoods. Most parents reported having at least one good friend in the neighborhood and talking on a regular basis with several adult and child neighbors. Many adults also participate in neighborhood organizations or activities. Although the Social Cohesion Index varies among neighborhoods, most respondents in each neighborhood reported that residents would intervene if they saw a problem occurring. This suggests a fairly high level of shared values and trust among neighbors, even in poorer areas such as East L.A.

> Once family income is held constant, children in all three neighborhoods are reported by parents to be doing equally well in school.

However, we also found that there are important differences in children's well-being among these three neighborhoods. Family income and other family characteristics explain part of the difference in outcomes, such as children's behavior and health. But these factors, important as they are, do not account for all of the differences in children's well-being among these neighborhoods. Even when differences in family income are factored out, kids in Windsor View appear to have significant advantages over kids in East L.A. As we noted earlier, poor kids in Windsor View—and, to a lesser extent, in Culver Marina—are better off than poor kids in East L.A. in terms of behavior problems and health status. Our study suggests that differences in neighborhood stability, safety, and social relations among neighbors may be part of the explanation.

As many of the people we talked to during the study told us, the effects of neighborhood life on children are complicated and tough to disentangle. As the study progressed, it became clear to us that other aspects of life in these neighborhoods, in addition to the ones we examined, affect kids' welfare. Policymakers and neighborhood residents alike want to know what those influences are, and we're in the process of finding out.

A broader look at L.A.

Our neighborhood study included only three communities. What we learned is tantalizing and suggestive, but three neighborhoods are not enough to develop general recommendations about the links between neighborhood characteristics and children's welfare.

To take the next step, we are conducting a large-scale survey of children living in 65 neighborhoods throughout Los Angeles County. We are following these children and their families over six years and interviewing them every three years. Our interviewers are also conducting systematic community observations, and we are interviewing local leaders, social service agencies, and business owners.

Our objective is to learn what aspects of family and neighborhood life make a difference for children growing up in Los Angeles. For example, is it better for children to grow up in neighborhoods where neighbors know each other and keep an eye on neighborhood children? Or are relationships among neighbors not particularly important for children in middle-class families? How important are neighborhood schools, parks, after-school programs, and playgrounds? Why do some neighborhoods improve substantially over time while others remain the same or deteriorate? Why do some families who live in violent and difficult neighborhoods raise well-adjusted children while other families are less successful? Why do some

kids who grow up in affluent neighborhoods and apparently happy families do poorly in school and develop behavior problems?

The study—called the Los Angeles Family and Neighborhood Survey (L.A.FANS)—is funded primarily by the National Institute of Child Health and Human Development (NICHD). More information about L.A.FANS and survey results are available on our web site (www.lasurvey.rand.org).

L.A.FANS will also provide information on several high-profile issues that Angelenos are concerned about, such as how to improve children's school readiness and early reading skills, changes in health insurance coverage for kids, family choices about child care and after-school care, factors contributing to rising asthma rates in children, and the effects of the reorganization of the Los Angeles Unified School District on the quality of education. For example, we will examine how the child care choices of poor and working-class families affect children's subsequent successes in school. We will also investigate why many poor, middle-class, and immigrant families still have no health insurance, despite new government initiatives.

The first stage of the L.A.FANS survey has just been completed. We are in the process of analyzing and compiling the results. Although it will take considerable time to fully understand these neighborhoods and families, results from these first interviews will be available over the next several months. We will prepare several types of reports, including access to the basic findings for L.A. County as a whole and each region of the county through our web site (www.lasurvey.rand.org), newspaper and magazine articles on neighborhoods and children's well-being to reach wider audiences, scientific publications for researchers and policymakers concerned about children, and presentations to nonprofit and government agencies.

The second stage of L.A.FANS is scheduled to begin in 2003. We will reinterview all families included in the first stage and also talk to families who are new to each neighborhood. This stage will let us examine how children and families are doing, whether neighborhoods have changed, and, if they have, why.

L.A.FANS will significantly enhance what we know about the complex and intimate interaction between children and the L.A. neighborhoods in which they live. We hope it will also help us understand this interaction in other neighborhoods beyond our backyard. ●

Endnotes

[1] Consult the suggested reading list for more information.

[2] Consult the suggested reading list for more information.

[3] Respondents were asked to rate their answers to the following questions on a scale of 1 (completely agree) to 4 (completely disagree): (a) We fight a lot in our family. (b) Family members almost never lose their calm. (c) Family members sometimes get so angry that they throw things. (d) Family members discuss their problems calmly. (e) Family members criticize each other a lot. (f) Family members sometimes hit each other. Responses have been recoded so that they all go in the same direction. Questions are taken from Sandra Hofferth, Pamela E. Davis-Kean, Jean Davis, and Jonathan Finkelstein, *The Child Development Supplement to the Panel Study of Income Dynamics: 1997 User Guide*, University of Michigan, 1999, http://www.isr.umich.edu/src/child-development/usergd.html.

[4] Robert J. Sampson, Jeffrey D. Morenoff, and Felton Earls, "Beyond Social Capital: Spatial Dynamics of Collective Efficacy for Children," *American Sociological Review*, Vol. 64, No. 5, October 1999, p. 33.

[5] See Brooks-Gunn, Duncan, and Aber, 1997.

[6] See Brooks-Gunn, Duncan, and Aber, 1997.

[7] See Los Angeles County Department of Health Services, *The Health of Angelenos: 2000*, www.lapublichealth.org/ha/.

[8] See Brooks-Gunn, Duncan, and Aber, 1997.

Suggestions for Further Reading

Brooks-Gunn, Jeanne, Greg J. Duncan, and J. Lawrence Aber, eds., *Neighborhood Poverty*, New York: The Russell Sage Foundation, 1997.

This two-volume book includes a thorough review of previous research on the consequences of neighborhood poverty for children's growth and development. It also reports new research on this topic by the authors.

Furstenberg, Frank F., and Mary Elizabeth Hughes, "Social Capital and Successful Development for At-Risk Youth," *Journal of Marriage and the Family*, Vol. 57, 1995, pp. 580–592.

This article describes the ways in which parents in poor communities try to make the best of the environment in which they and their children live.

Jacobs, Jane, *The Death and Life of Great American Cities*, New York: Random House, 1961.

This is a classic study and critique of urban development that describes the function and importance of neighborhoods for urban dwellers.

Sampson, Robert J., "Neighborhoods and Violent Crime: A Multilevel Study of Collective Efficacy," *Science*, Vol. 277, No. 5328, August 15, 1997, p. 918.

This article presents findings of a study in Chicago on the role of the social environment on youth violence. We used some of the same measures of social environment in our study.

Wellman, Barry, and Scot Wortley, "Different Strokes from Different Folks: Community Ties and Social Support," *American Journal of Sociology*, Vol. 96, 1990, pp. 558–588.

An in-depth analysis of the importance of social networks in communities.

Methods Used in the Focused Study of Children and Neighborhoods

We interviewed neighborhood residents using standard social survey interview techniques. In each household, we interviewed the adult who had primary responsibility for taking care of the children. In most but not all households, this was the mother. We asked questions about the neighborhood, family life, and the well-being of one of the children in the household. The child was chosen at random from all children (under age 18) living in the household.

The sample for the household survey was drawn as follows. We obtained and cross-checked address lists for each of the three census tracts from commercial sources. Addresses were then selected at random from these lists. We sent each selected household a letter outlining the purposes of the study and asking for their help. Interviewers then visited each household to determine if it was eligible for interview. Only households that included children under 18 years old were eligible. We completed 30 interviews in Culver Marina, 32 in East L.A., and 29 in Windsor View. The results discussed in this book were based on a sample of 91 children and their families.